You and Me

I Can Play Fairly

Angela Leeper

Heinemann Library

Chicago, Illinois

© 2005 Heinemann Library,
a division of Reed Elsevier, Inc.
Chicago, Illinois

Customer Service 888-454-2279
Visit our website at www.heinemannlibrary.com

Designed by Mike Hogg (Maverick)
Printed and bound in China by South China Printing Company Limited
Photo research by Janet Lankford Moran

09 08 07 06 05
10 9 8 7 6 5 4 3 2 1

Library of Congress Cataloging-in-Publication Data
Leeper, Angela.
  I Can Play Fairly / Angela Leeper.
      p. cm. – (You and me)
Includes index.
ISBN 1-4034-6075-2(HC), ISBN 1-4034-6083-3 (Pbk.)
1. Sportsmanship--Juvenile literature I.Title. II. Series
GV706.3.L44 2004
175.22

2004016613

Acknowledgments
The author and publisher are grateful to the following for permission to reproduce copyright material:
Cover photograph by Norbert Schaefer/Corbis
p. 4 Ariel Skelley/Corbis; p. 5 Tony Freeman/Photo Edit, Inc.; pp. 6, 16, 17 Warling Studios/Heinemann Library; p. 7 Ty Allison/Taxi/Getty Images; pp. 8, 15 David Young-Wolff/Photo Edit, Inc.; p. 9 Cindy Charles/Photo Edit, Inc.; p. 10 Chris Cole/The Image Bank/Getty Images; p. 11 Robert W. Ginn/Photo Edit, Inc.; p. 12 Ryan McVay/Photodisc Green/Getty Images; p. 13 Raeanne Rubenstein/Index Stock Imagery; p. 13 Robert W. Ginn/Photo Edit, Inc.; p. 14 Cassy Cohen/Photo Edit, Inc.; p. 18 Charles Gupton/Corbis; p. 19 SW Productions/Brand X Pictures/Getty Images; pp. 20, 21, 22, 23 Janet Moran/Heinemann Library; back cover (L-R) Warling Studios/Heinemann Library, Charles Gupton/Corbis

Every effort has been made to contact copyright holders of any material reproduced in this book.
Any omissions will be rectified in subsequent printings if notice is given to the publisher.

Many thanks to the teachers, library media specialists, reading instructors, and educational consultants who have helped develop the Read and Learn brand.

Contents

What Is Playing Fairly?

Playing fairly means you follow the rules of the game.

Playing fairly is not about winning.

You try your best and have fun.

Where Can You Play Fairly?

You can play fairly at home.

You can play fairly at school, too.

You can play fairly in the park.

You can play fairly on a sports team.

Why Do You Play Fairly?

You play fairly because you want to have fun.

You want to be fair to everyone who is playing.

You want your teammates to have fun, too.

What Does It Look Like When You Play Fairly?

When you play fairly, you shake hands.

You may also smile.

Whether you win or lose, you can shake hands with the other players.

What Does It Sound Like When You Play Fairly?

You may hear someone say, "Good job!"

You may hear clapping hands, too.

Whether you win or lose, you can say "Good job!" to the other team.

How Can You Play Fairly at Home?

When you play a game you follow the rules.

If you lose a game, you do not get angry.

You can try and win another time.

How Can You Play Fairly at School?

You can take turns when you play at school.

When you play fairly everyone gets a chance to play.

How Can You Play Fairly in Sports?

You can listen to the coach.

He tells you the rules of the game.

When you play fairly you can clap
for the other team.

How Do You Feel When You Play Fairly?

You can feel good when you play fairly.

You know you tried your best.

Quiz

How can you play fairly?

Answer to Quiz

You can follow the rules.

You can take turns.

Note to Parents and Teachers

Reading for information is an important part of a child's literacy development. Learning begins with a question about something. Help children think of themselves as investigators and researchers by encouraging their questions about the world around them. Each chapter in this book begins with a question. Read the question together. Look at the pictures. Talk about what you think the answer might be. Then read the text to find out if your predictions were correct. Think of other questions you could ask about the topic, and discuss where you might find the answers. Assist children in using the picture glossary and the index to practice new vocabulary and research skills.

Index